The Road
to Arrowhead

Adam Blue

Stone House Press
247 Burr Road
Cornish, NH 03745

First Printing, 2016

ISBN: 153007669
ISBN-13: 978-1530076697

This book is lovingly dedicated to my family,
from whom it's been hidden until this point.

For a California boy, New England winters are dark, perilously so. Dark unto the point of distraction, even from the things you love, if that's the right word.

By way of example, I had recently exchanged texts with a professional acquaintance about the possibility of having a show in his gallery, and it sounded like we could make it happen in the new year. Exciting! Though we hadn't worked together in the past, we always made time to chat at local functions and even caught a casual beer or two standing by a grill in the summertime. He was familiar with my work and had inquired if I had anything new cooking. I sent him some images of the series I was developing, a project about rural life, its hardships and occasional celebrations. All positives, right?

Well, when it's dark and cold every damn day, my energy flags. Add to this feeling deadlines looming and personal responsibilities doubling down—it's the weight of the world. All of it. Massive and burdensome. My actions thrash against the tide to little effect. So rather than sink, I succumb to the Internet. The temptation to wade into one-thousand-and-one clicks is its own salve. It's working without working, the psychological experience of being busy with neither investment nor accomplishment.

One January Thursday, things were feeling particularly grim and my focus drifted listlessly. The news websites I frequented proffered the latest litany of catastrophes, every clickbait lede supported by bluster peppered with ads. I re-re-checked my email, an act more pathetic than wishing food from the expiring corn starch and ketchup malingering in the pantry. So I navigated to eBay, the ever-present exhibition of trash hoping to be treasure.

And here I admit, when confronted by feelings of personal, professional, and political powerlessness, I shop online—as though conjuring an object from desire to doorstep wasn't a surrogate for my failing will-to-power.

My latest obsession is vintage men's watches. Specifically, India's HMT mass-consumer line from the 1970s. I covet them. The designs are gorgeous, the numbering sublime. And the online marketplace is flooded, with hundreds available for as little as ten bucks. But I can't make myself buy one. I'm convinced that from the surplus, the watch I choose will be damaged to its core, that its antiquated hand-winding mechanism won't even keep time. And in a blink, the Internet does what it does best—alchemically mixing curiosity with apathy to yield voyeurism, frustration, and guilt.

§

Sensing there was no bottom to the developing pattern, I forced my own hand. I contacted my gallerist friend and scheduled a follow-up lunch. Thus compelled, I needed to advance my project beyond our last conversation, to demonstrate that I was serious about maximizing an exhibition in his space. So, breaking from my dawdling habit, I searched online for picture frames.

I entered our lunch feeling prepared. I left renewed, blood pumping. The rush of exposure, it's like an addiction. Early in my career, having an exhibition felt essential, felt the natural culmination of a sequence of events that reached their peak with friends old and new. I'd seek out others' impressions of my work to change my understanding, my motivations. I'd amend my process accordingly, and feel perhaps that the viewers had been influenced, too. But you get old. And slowly then suddenly, showing becomes the cost of doing business. And swimming in that sea of confidants, it remains a pleasure until the moment when, through laziness or efficiency, you hear yourself parrot your own choice clichés, rehashing the tales you've told before to desired outcomes—courting consumers, courting commerce, being the business person you hoped to avoid by choosing the arts. The pleasure is numbing, the pleasure is work. In any event, a friendship was forming. There was new art to share. The spark was still there.

But framing. Fucking framing. The piling on of an additional layer of labor after the work is done. Having to delineate gilt boundaries that subjugate the art. The edge, always trying to trump the center. This final creative negotiation serves only the viewer. And the expense. Bloody hell. Making art takes so much of you—time, effort, focus, love. And then the burden of framing on top of that! With enough experience, you adjust your expectation, building this final step into your process so there's no surprise. But damn it's expensive, even if you pass it on to the customer at the point of sale.

So I continued clicking around eBay, and one morning, there they were. Just what I needed. A batch lot of frames, consistent of size and quality, cheap, and best—no other bidders.

§

The seller's profile hailed from Arrowhead, West Virginia, just outside of Weston. Their history revealed completed sales of low-value kitsch randomness, esoteric objects you might find featured on one of those abandoned-storage-unit-auction reality TV shows, or maybe one about hoarders. Commemorative plates. Water-damaged athletic cards. The odd musical instrument, dented but in its original case.

The listing wasn't even for frames. eBay's algorithm sent me to framed artworks, too. I squinted at a collection of prints salvaged from a shuttered motel. The photographs the seller provided were of amateur quality: yellow incandescent lighting, the product placed haphazardly on a wrinkled sheet laid across a living-room couch. The artwork itself was typical, innocuous hotel fare—derivative, off-label Audubon-style prints of birds. Decades of continuous display had worn them down. The mats were deteriorating. The cheap paper buckled at the edges. Some prints had slipped their mounting tape, presenting themselves off-kilter. The poor-quality inks had faded inconsistently, casting what remained sickly oranges, greens, reds, browns, and blues.

None of this mattered to me. In fact, it was a boon, as it distracted other viewers from the frames themselves. They were all the same size, all the same profile: the wooden set was a uniform 13" x 17". A little bevel as modest ornamentation. They were mottled silver, with dings here and there. They all had glass. I figured I'd have to touch them up, spray paint at the least. The entire lot had a "Buy It Now" price of $30, and there were no bids. Shipping would be another $30 if it went on the slow boat, bringing the total to $60 for 30 frames. There's my next show.

I noted the time the sale would end and copied the URL into a word doc for later reference. Figuring a bid may attract other buyers, I clicked away with the resolve to return for the closing minutes. The auction remained a dead zone in the interim, barren of any demonstrated interest. I offered $10 and went on my way.

§

The boxes came three weeks later, arriving during a perfect storm of hassle. Multiple deadlines at work conspired to land on the same day, pulling late evenings and early mornings into the mix. My social media were an unrelenting obituary column. The wood-stove flue broke the day after the hot-water heater's ignition switch failed. And my old dog developed a new pattern, whimpering with askance eyes until she'd retch on the carpet by my bed, every night at three. I'd feel rage, if it weren't for the exhaustion.

I stashed the frames down cellar, the boxes unopened, insulated by the dark and cold until things settled down.

§

Come spring, the exhibition was foremost on my mind. I'd completed forty ink drawings on schedule, revealing a network of individuals and opinions—a community in crisis, really—that I hoped was both empathetic and tense. With two-weeks remaining before install, I collected the frames from the basement and began staging the show.

I cleaned my studio ahead of time, moving the clutter to the walls. I put a folding table in the middle of the room, loading it with an exact-o, sandpaper, paint, paper towels, and windex. I popped the shipping tape on the first box. The seller had crated them well, with cardboard between each piece. I was relieved to find none of the glass had broken in transit.

I pulled the first frame from the box and froze with fear. I grabbed for a second, dropping it on top of the first. A third. A fourth. I raked everything aside and spilled the entire contents of the box across the table. Like twisted playing cards, they shuffled before my eyes. I bolted for the door, running to be cleansed by the sun, gasping for fresh air. The walls had collapsed around me. I didn't go back to the studio for three days.

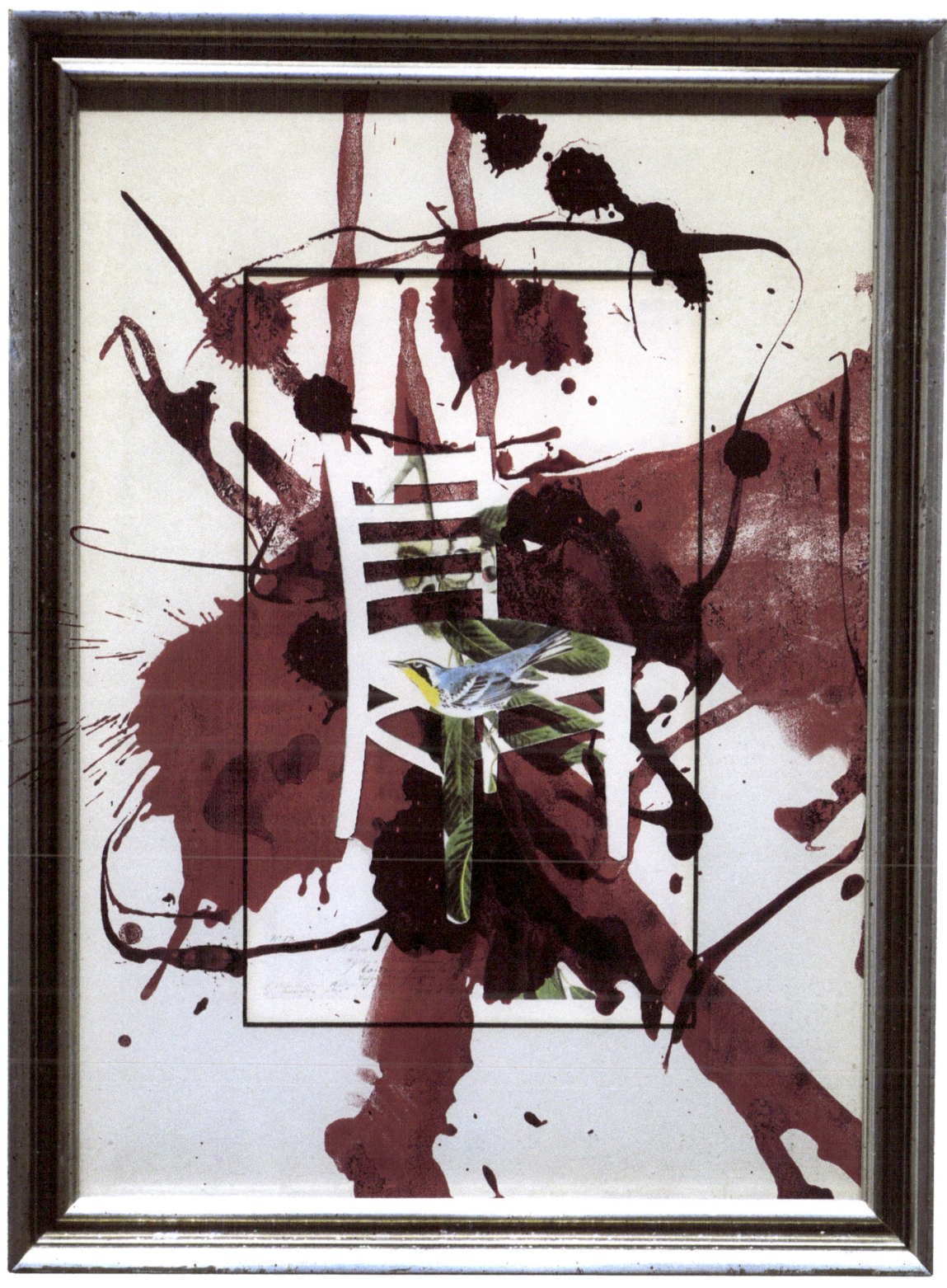

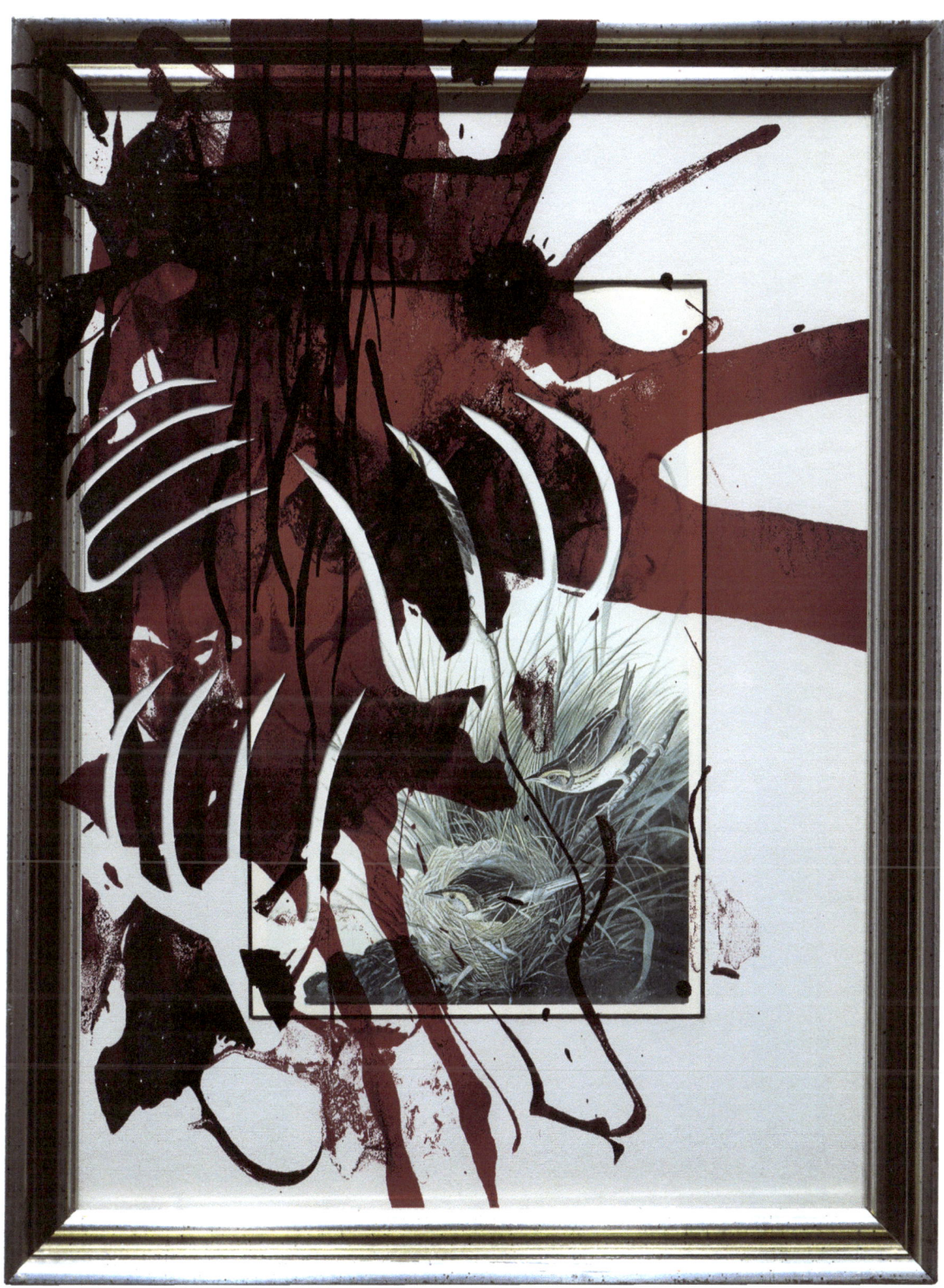

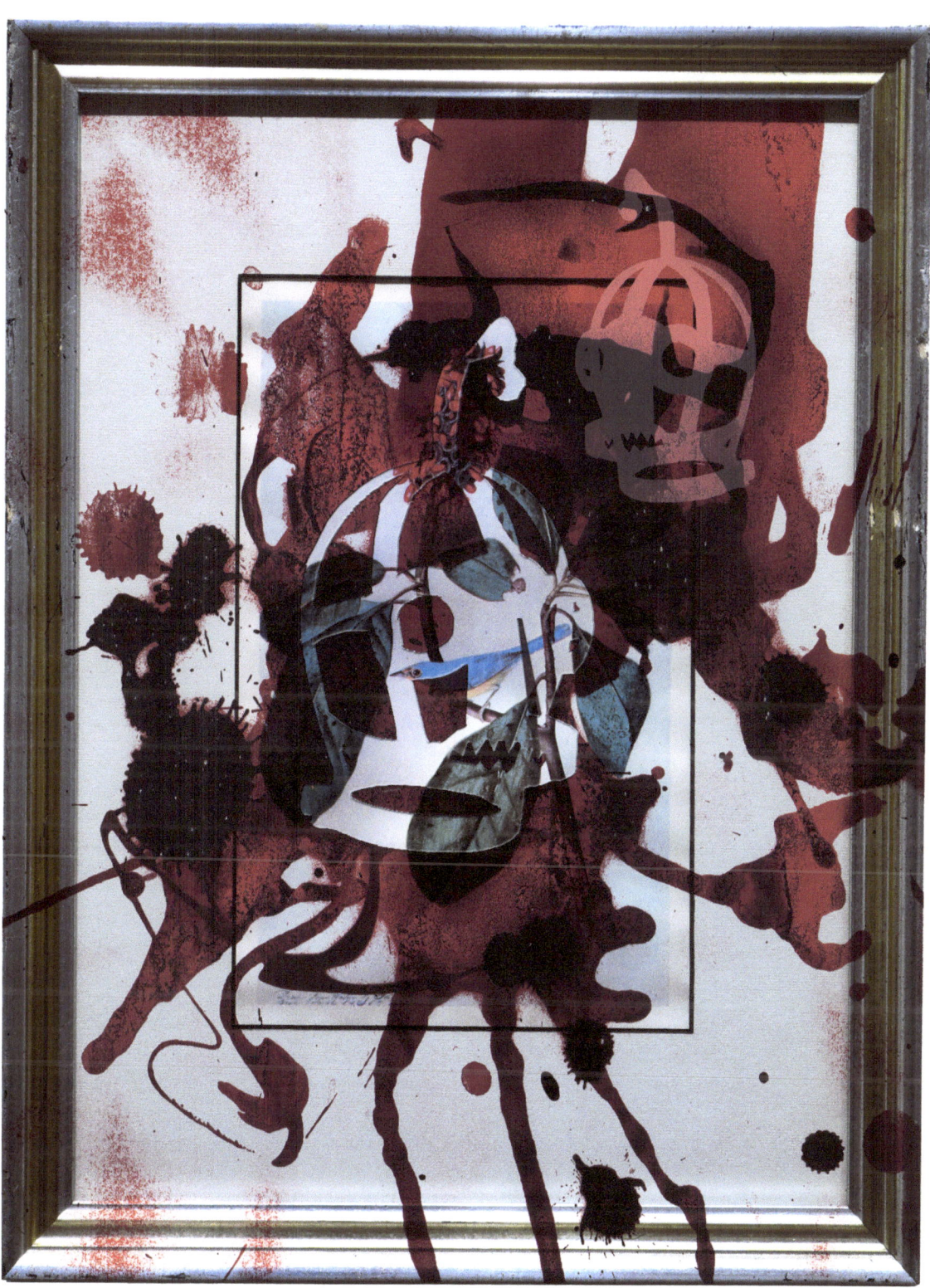

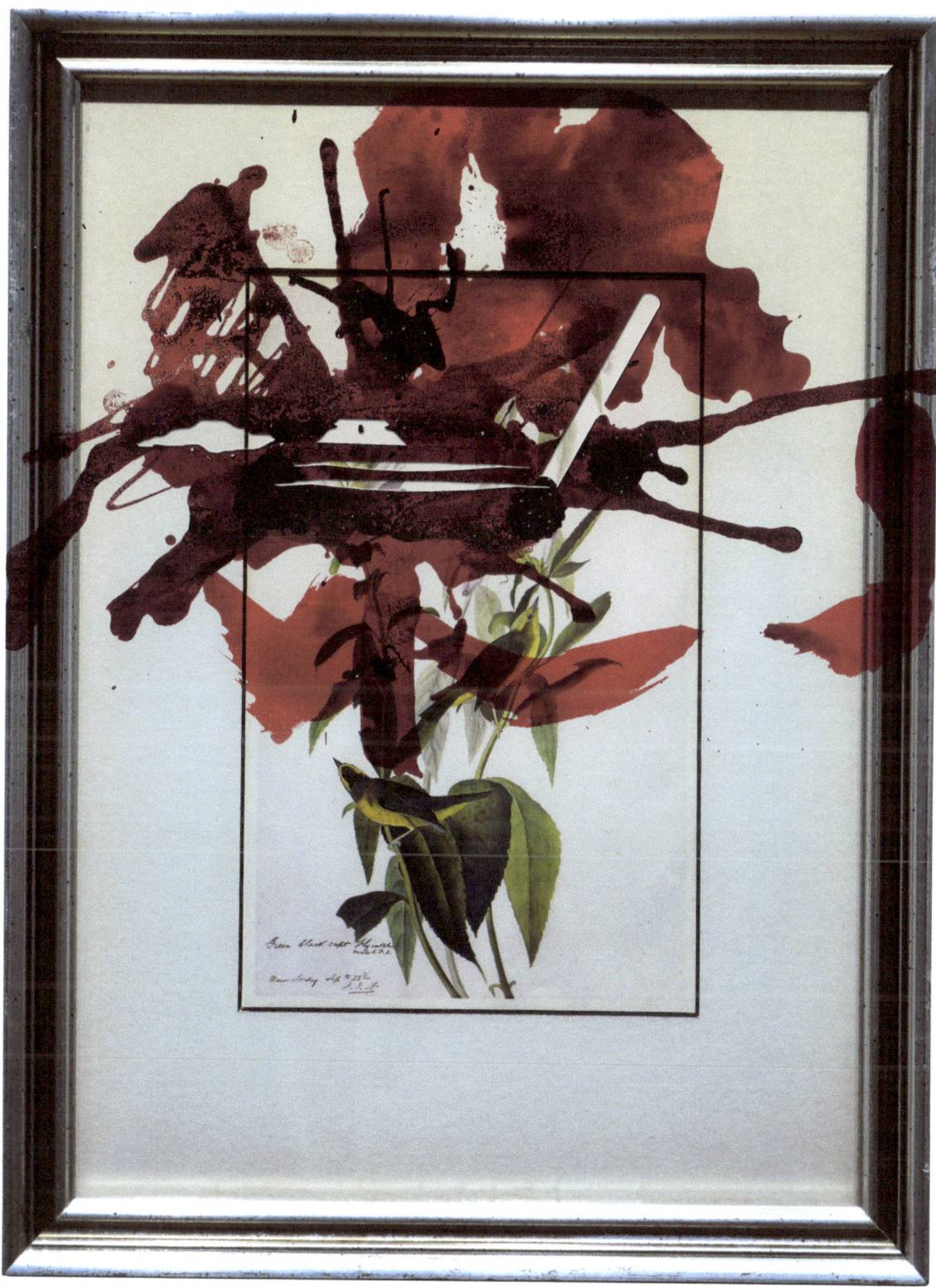

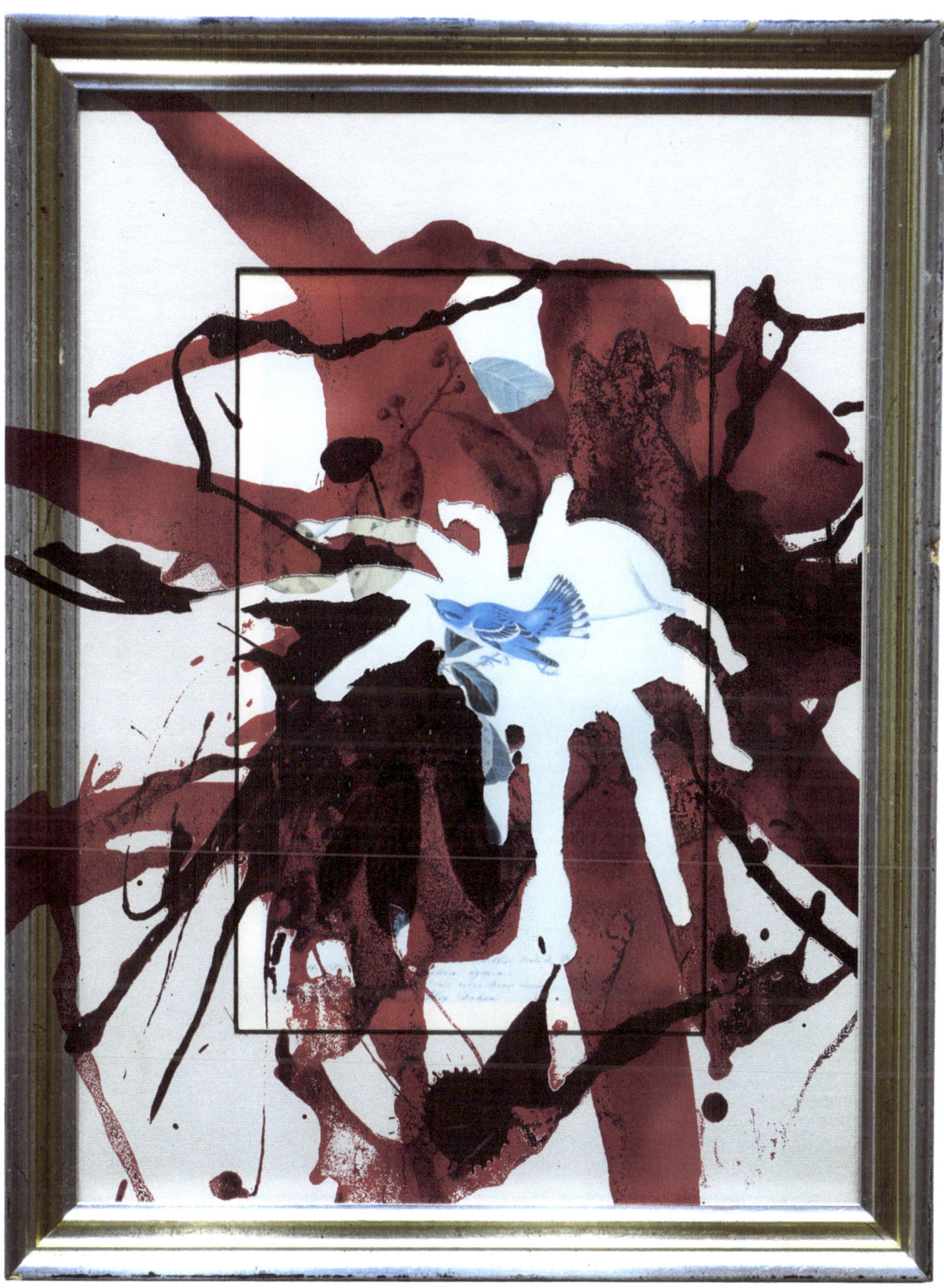

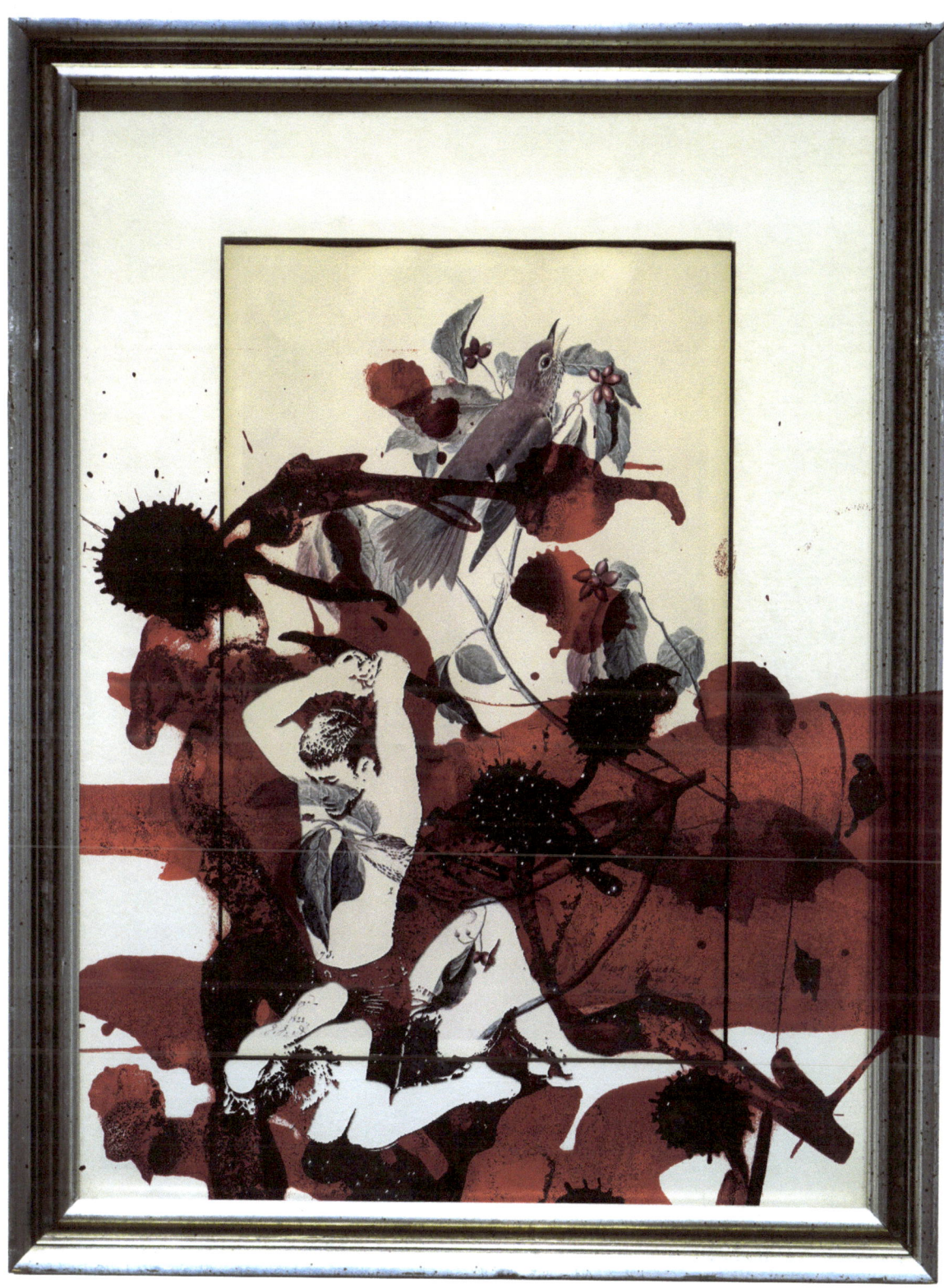

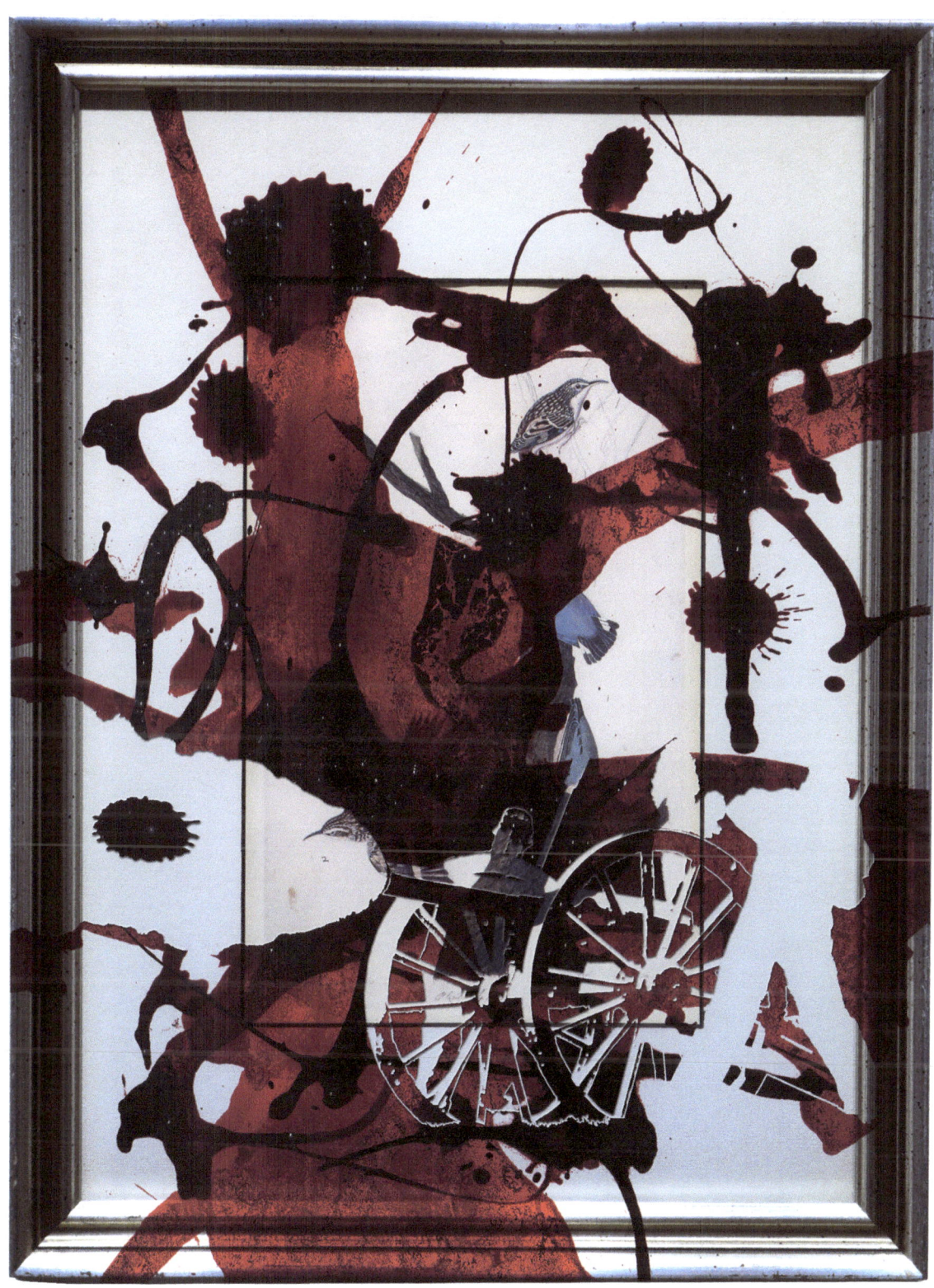

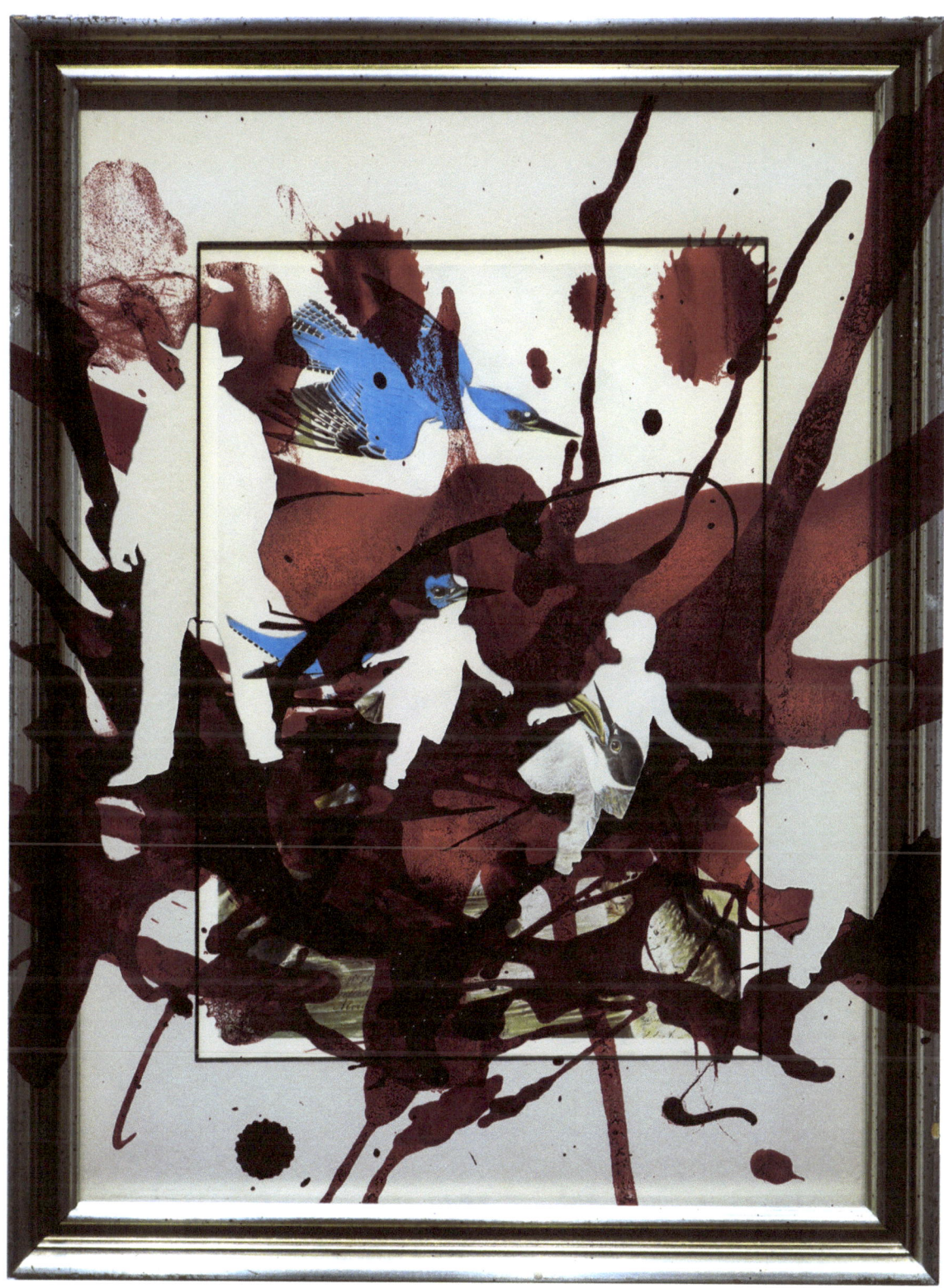

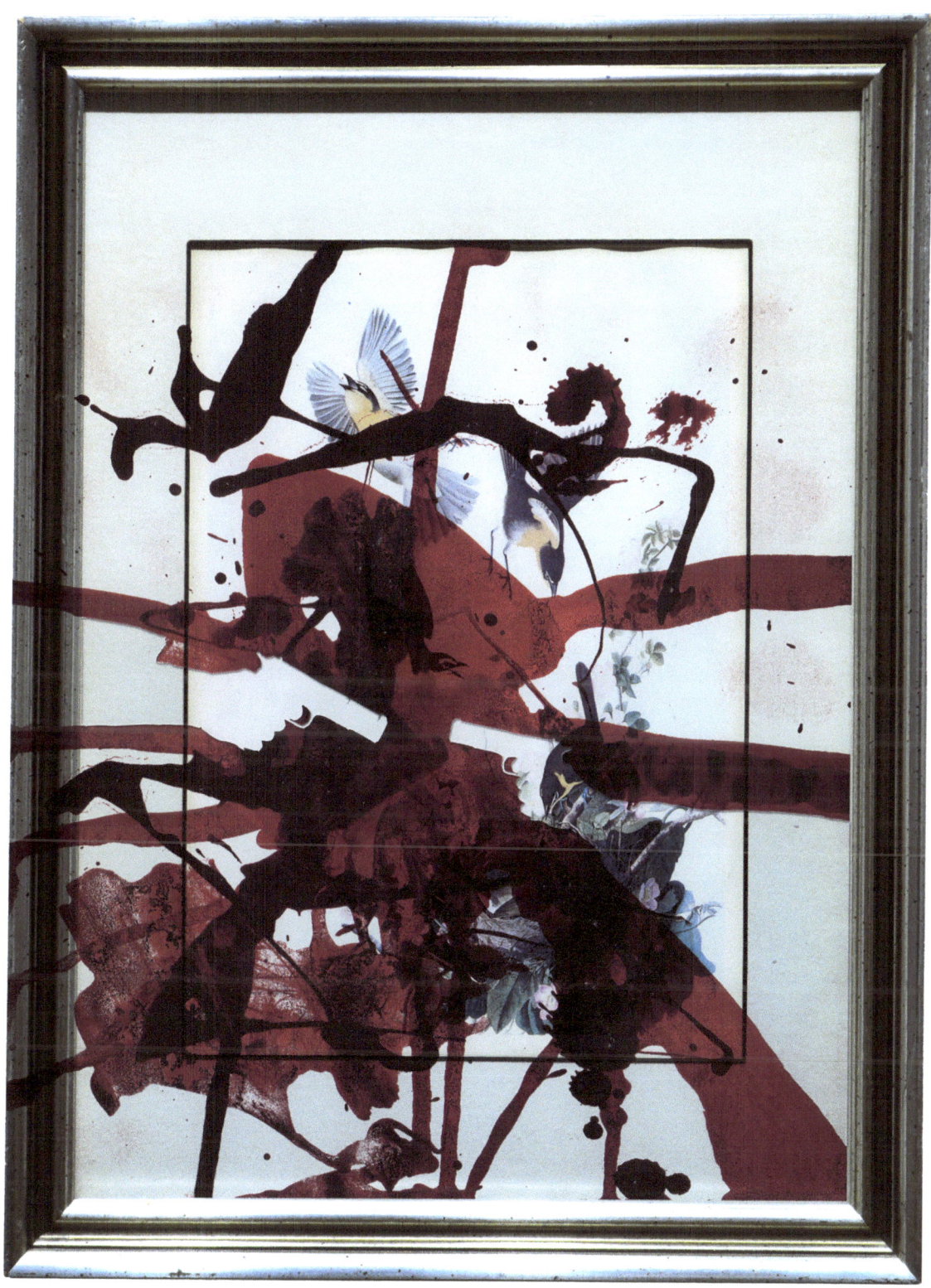

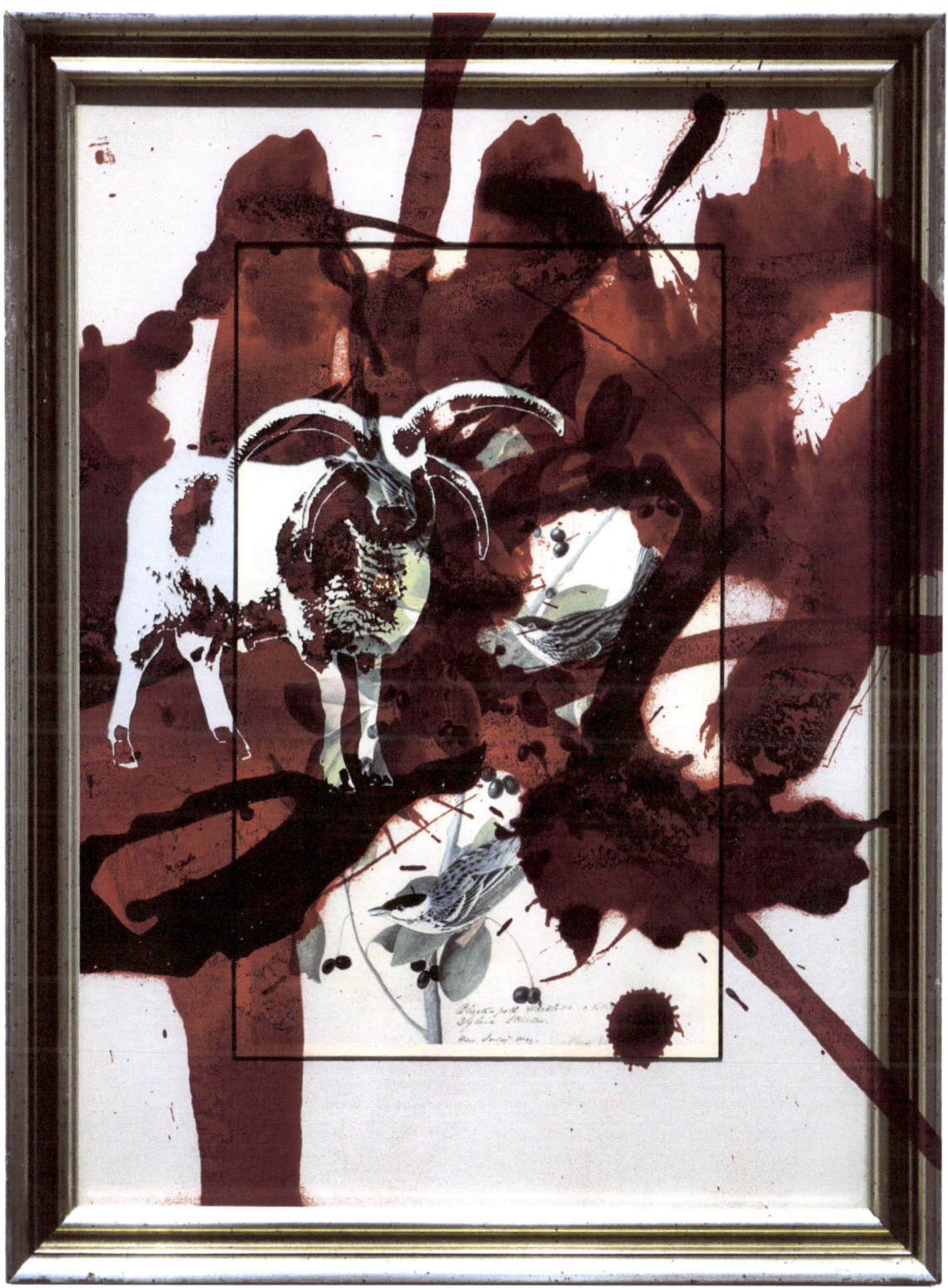

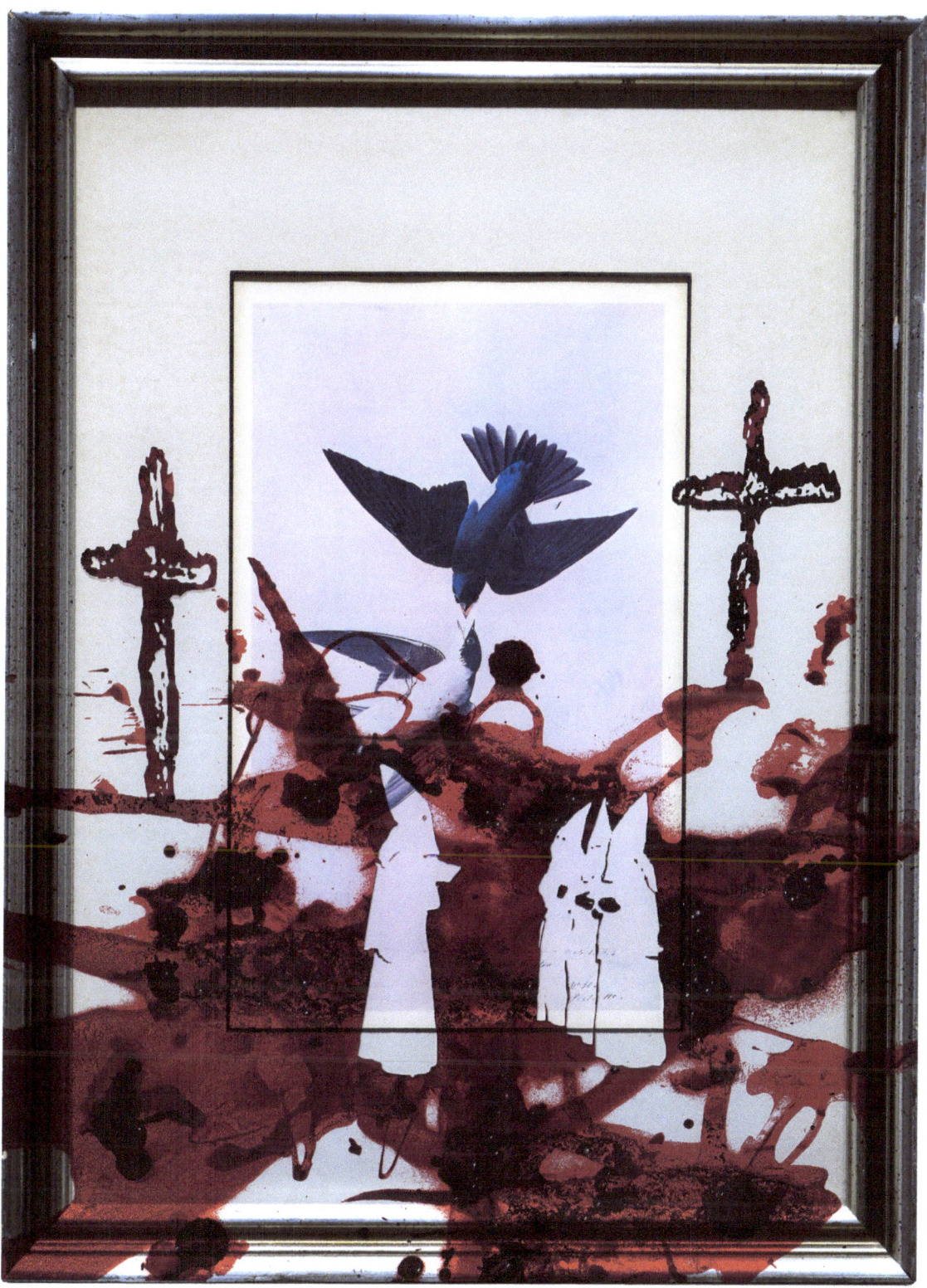

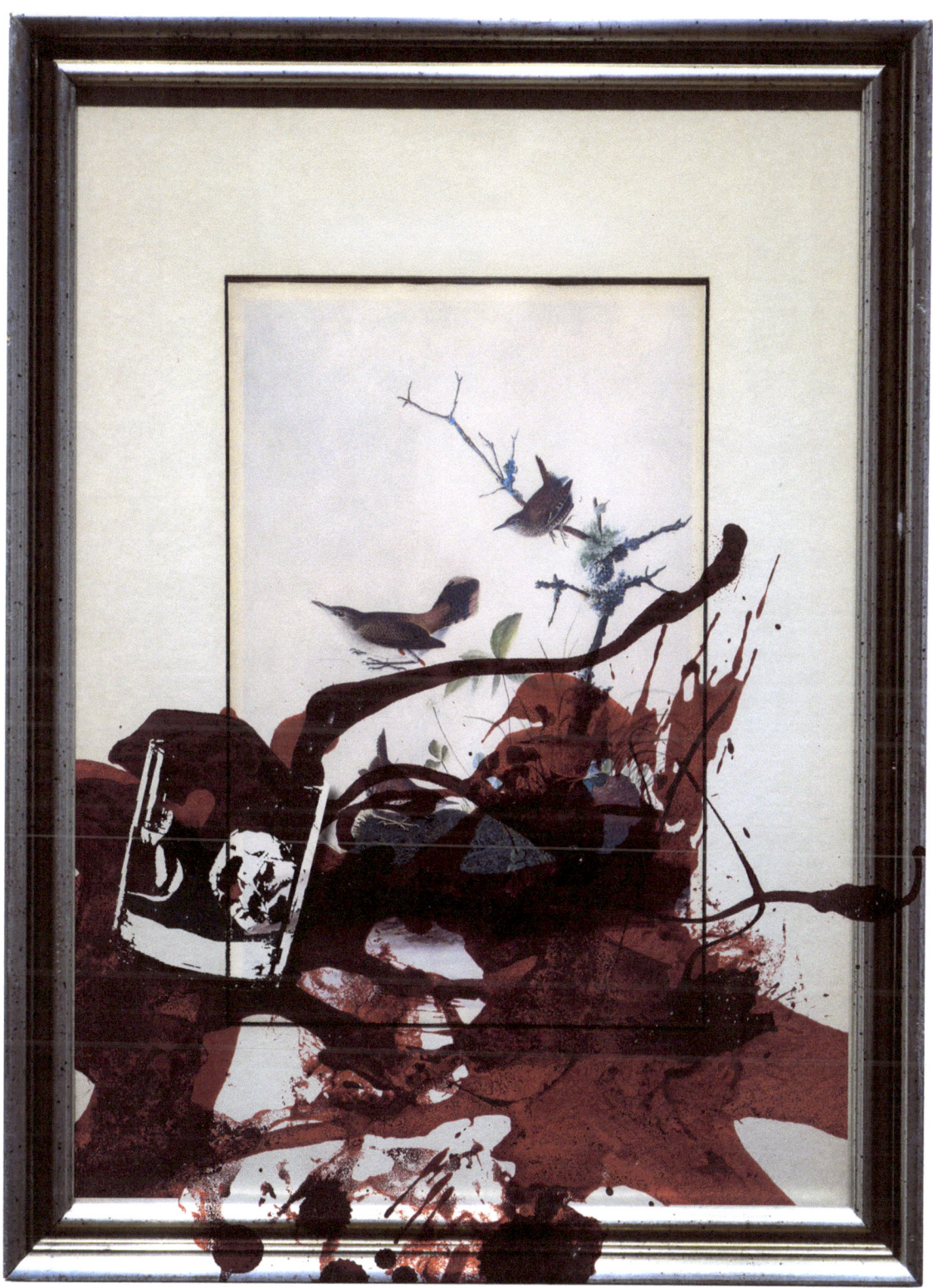

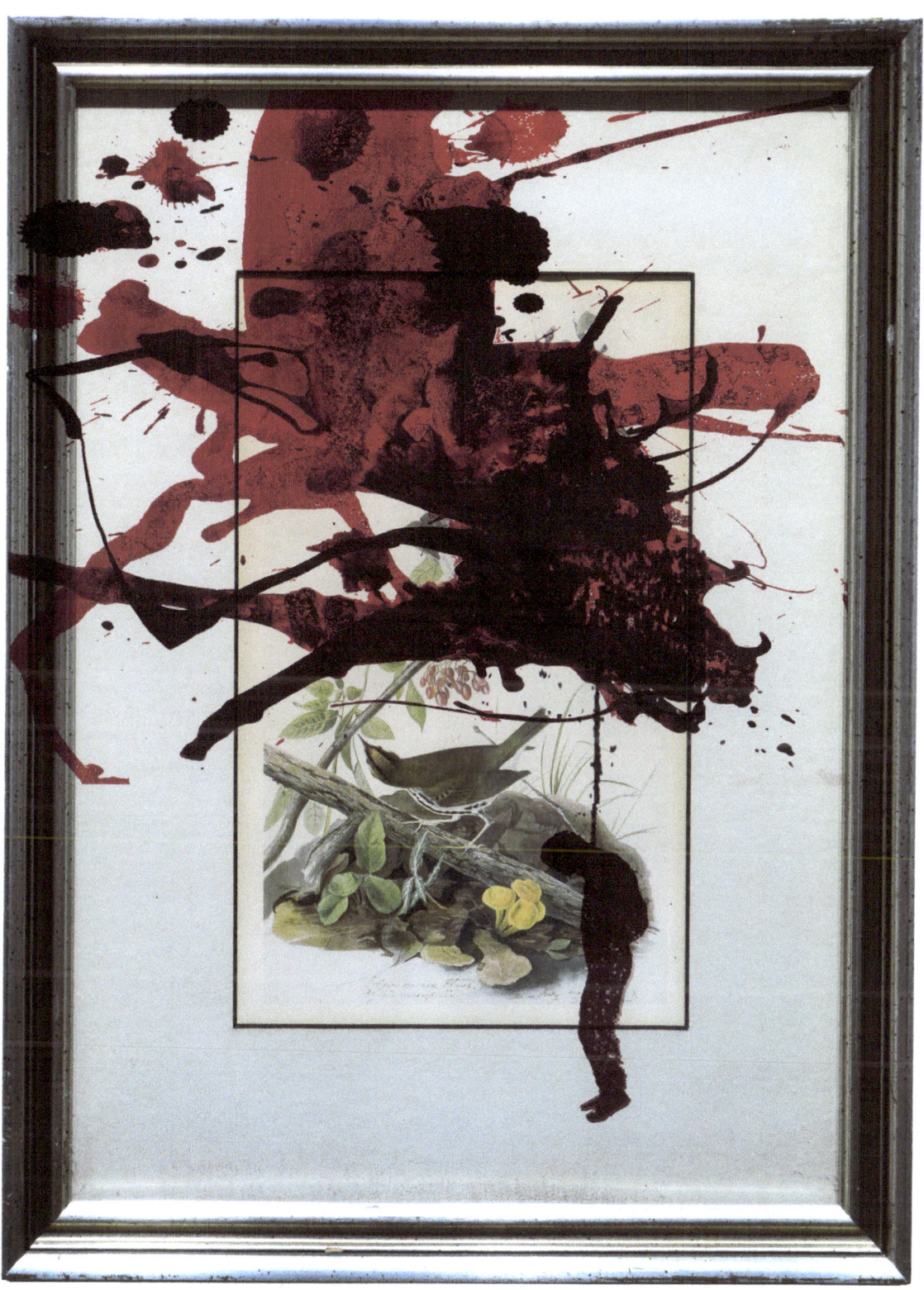

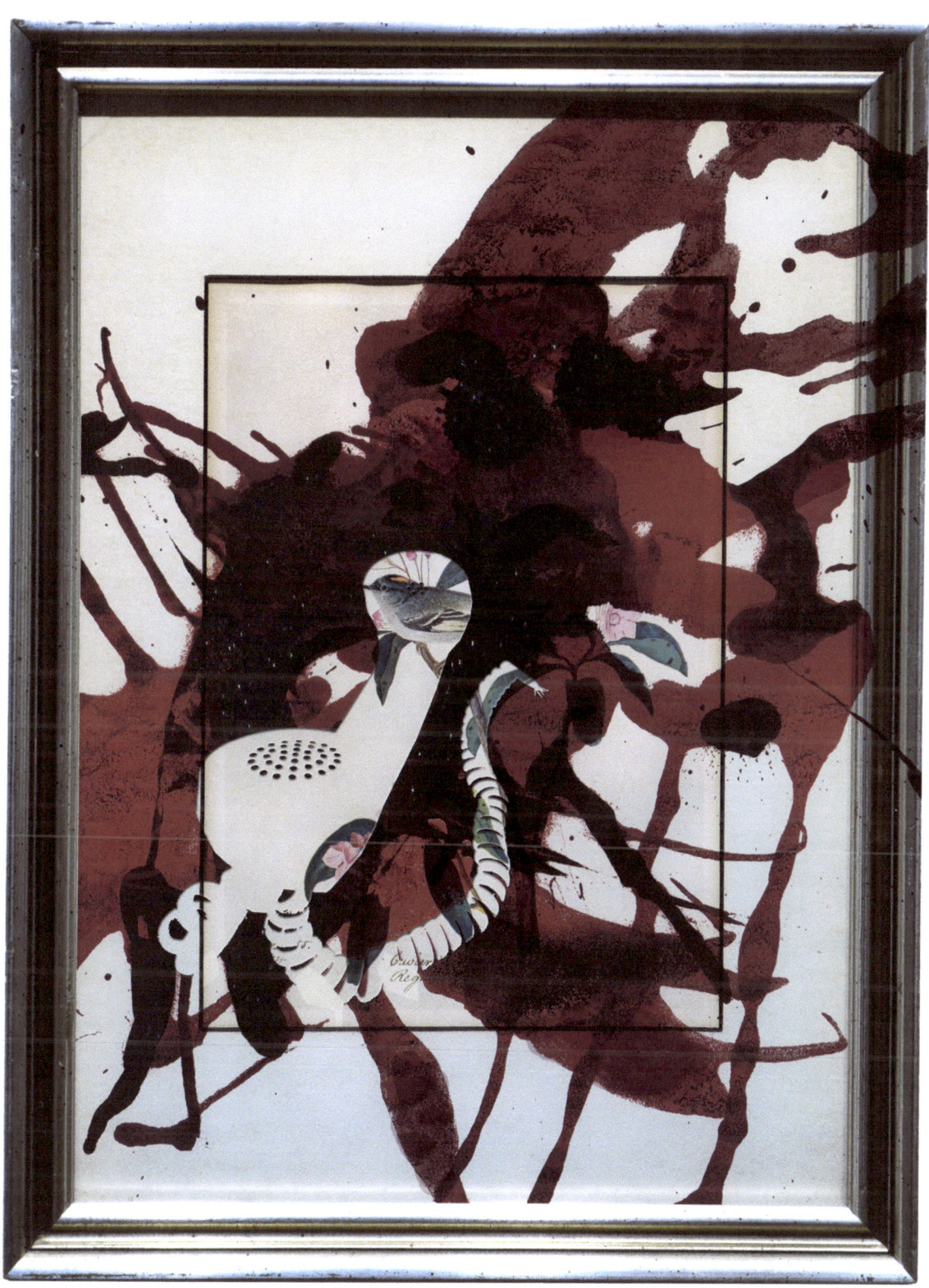

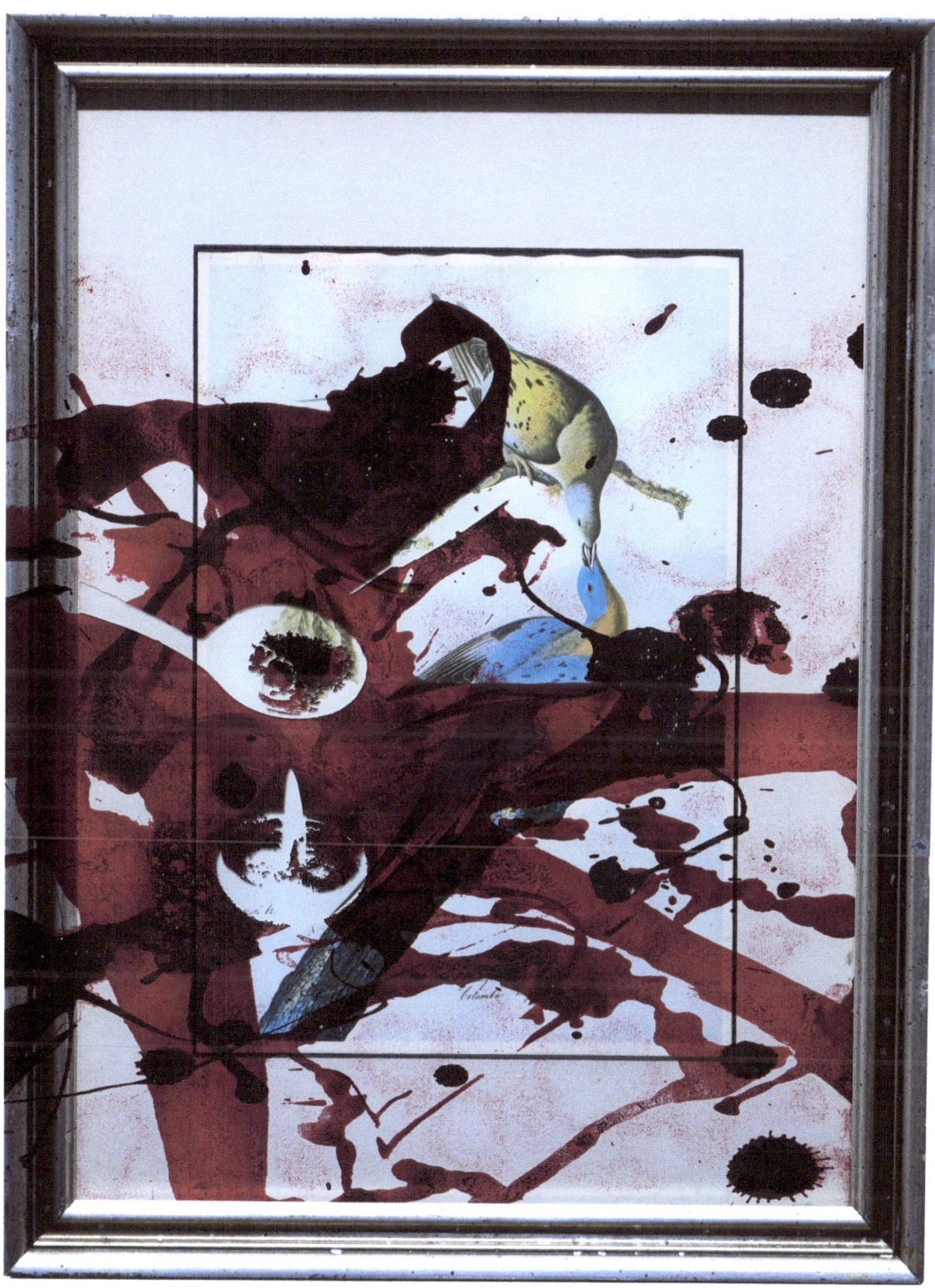

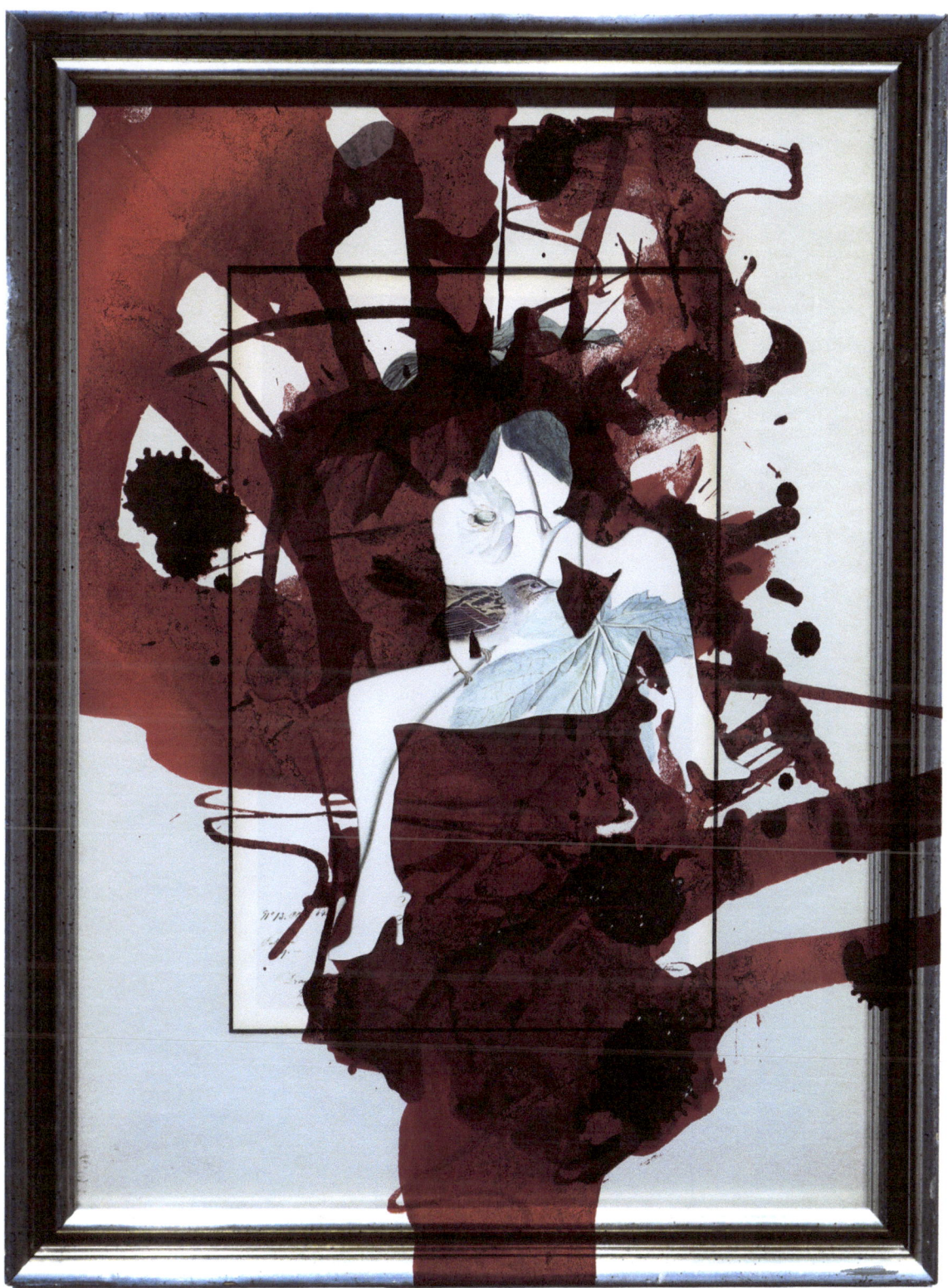

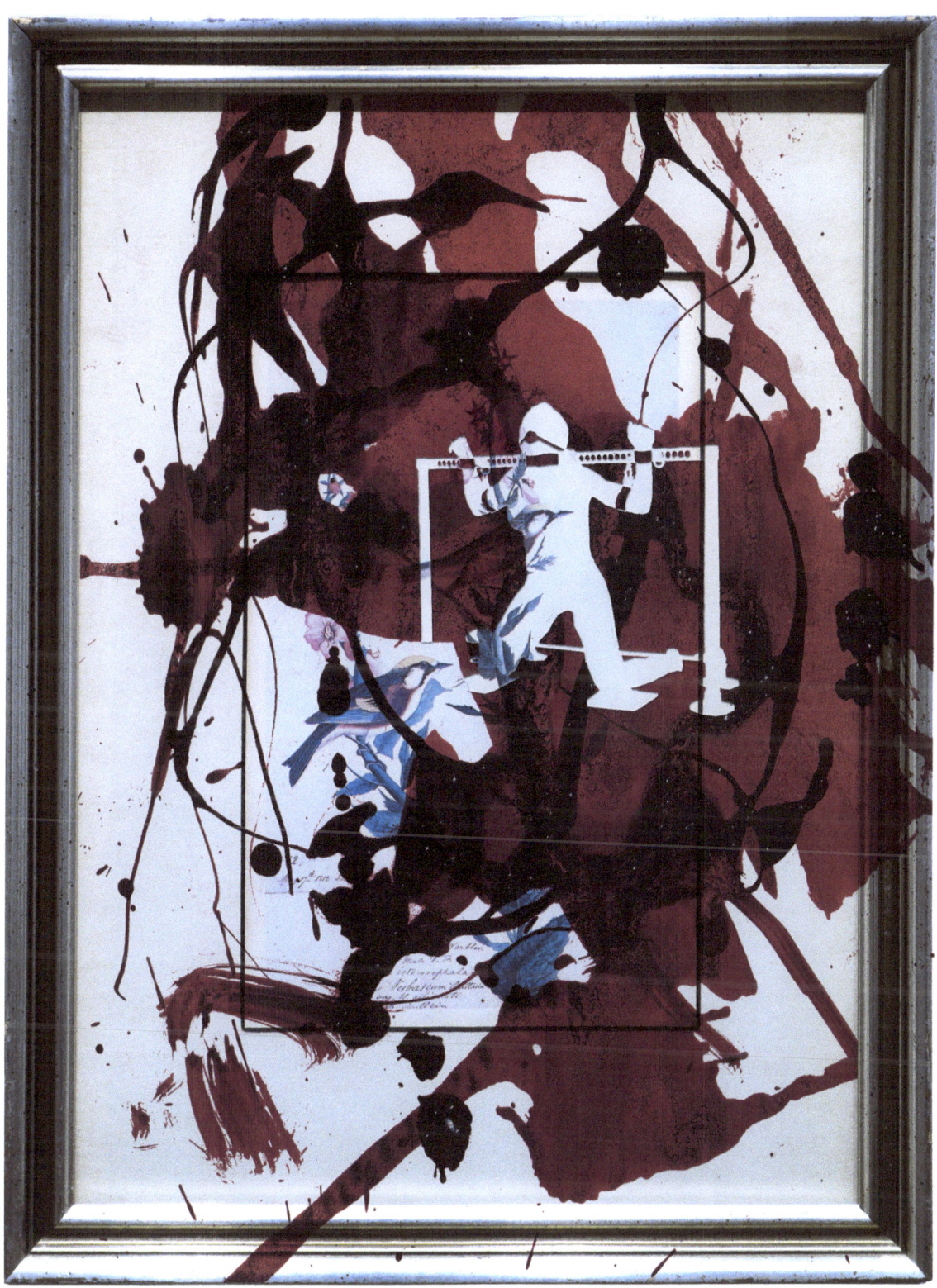

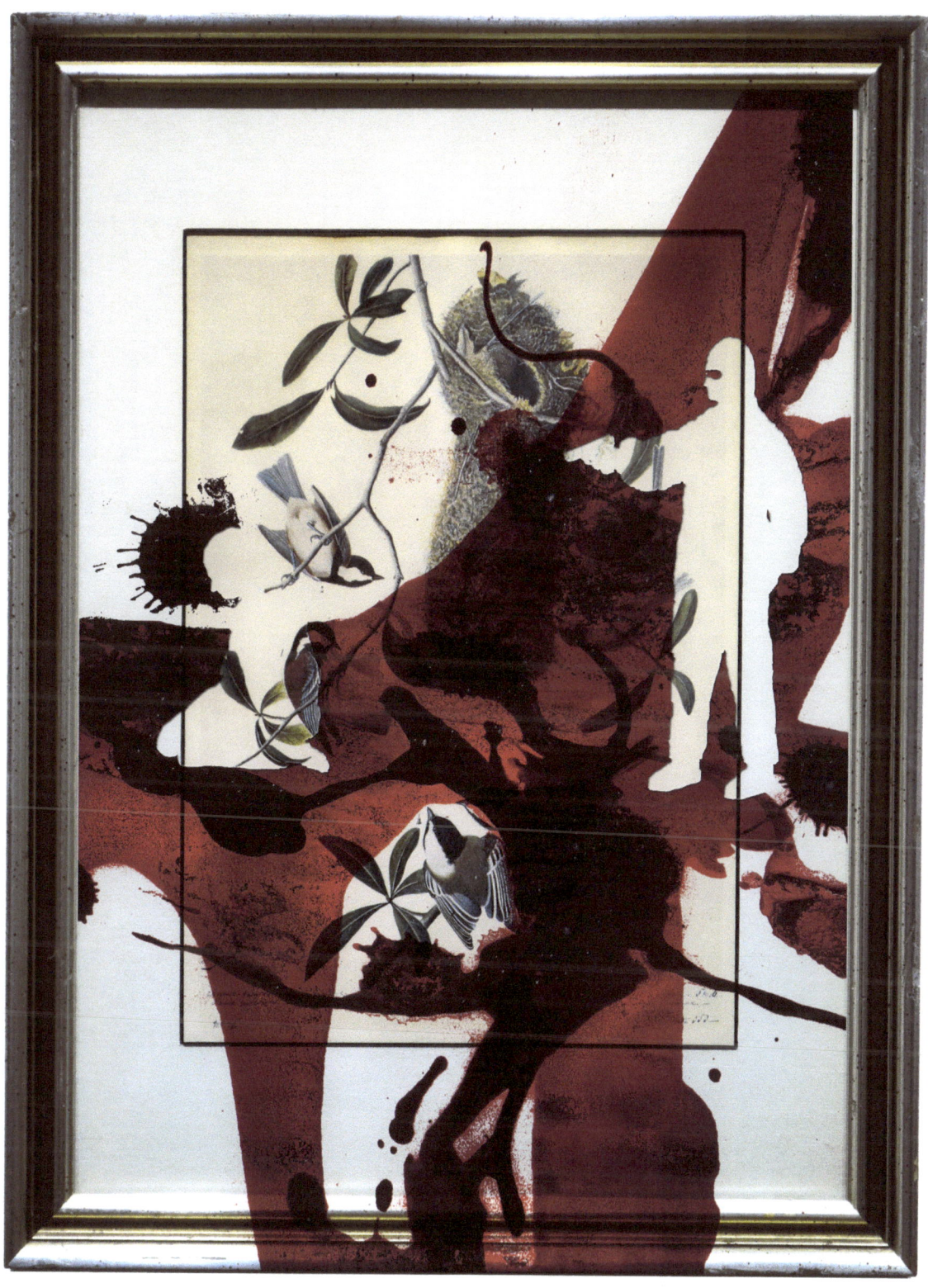

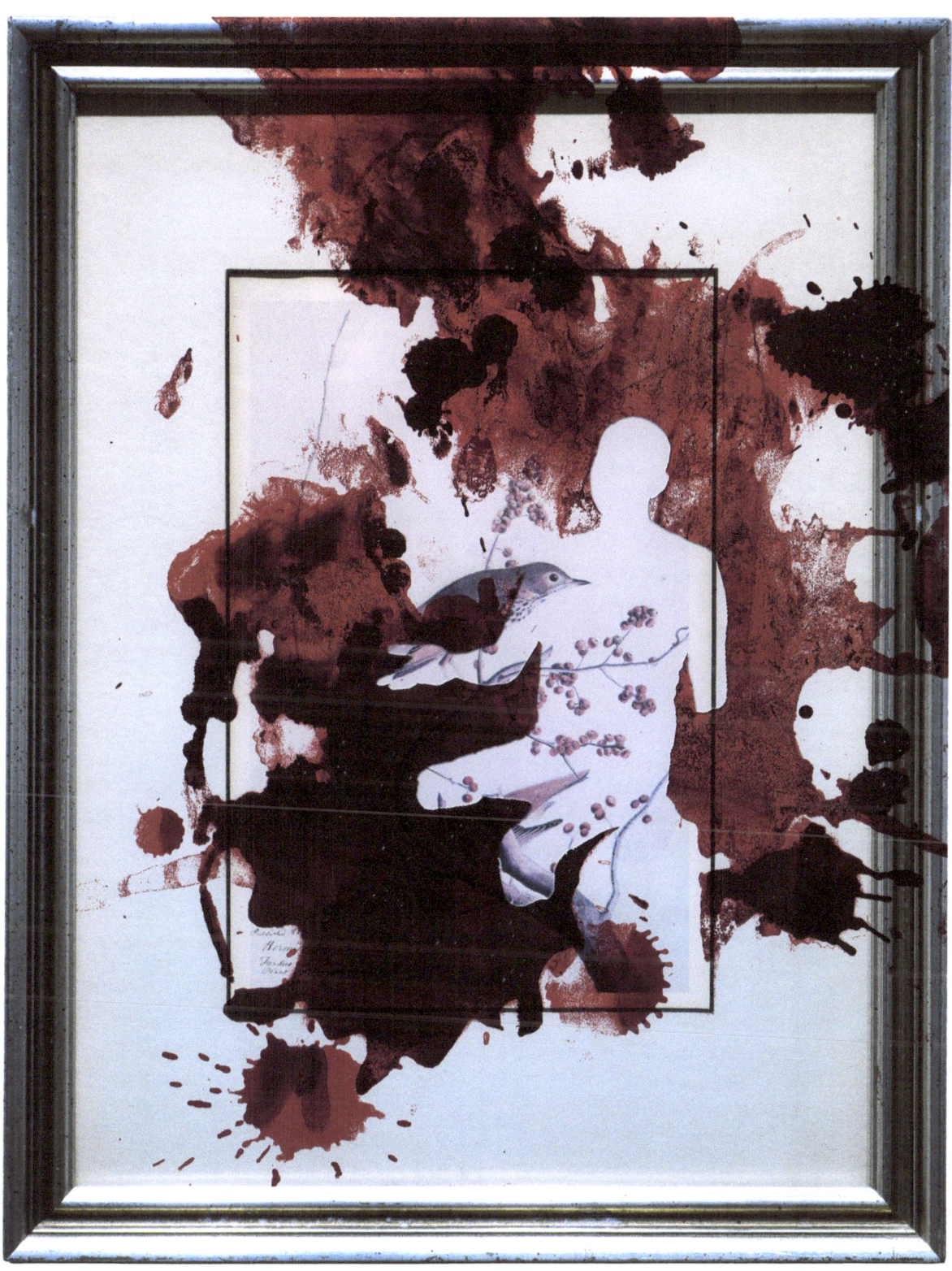

I booted up my computer and logged onto eBay. The seller's profile was inactive, stuck in virtual purgatory since our transaction.

I researched the history of Arrowhead, West Virginia, looking for links to articles about motel closings in the past year. I sought stories about economic developments, both up and down. Names, any names, that might shed light on what came into my house. I went to Google Maps, wandering the small town in street view. I navigated to the Internet Archive, wandering google maps again, this time in 2014, then 2012 — looking for any changes in the landscape.

Arrowhead had a paper, *The Beacon*, from which I gleaned that the town originated as an offshoot of Weston, providing lower rents for the families that had been priced out of Weston's relative financial strength.

It was then I first stumbled upon the rise and fall of one of Weston's primary economic engines—the Trans-Allegheny Lunatic Asylum. The following description is a lightly edited copy of what appears on Wikipedia:

> The Trans-Allegheny Lunatic Asylum was authorized by the Virginia General Assembly in the early 1850s. A building was designed in the Gothic Revival and Tudor Revival styles, and construction began in late 1858. Work was initially conducted by prison laborers; a local newspaper noted "seven convict negroes" as the first arrivals for work. Skilled stonemasons were later brought in from Germany and Ireland.
>
> Construction was interrupted by the Civil War in 1861. Following its secession from the United States, the government of Virginia demanded the return of the hospital's unused construction funds. Before this could occur, the 7th Ohio Volunteer Infantry seized the money from a local bank. It was put toward the establishment of the Reorganized Government of Virginia, which sided with the northern states.
>
> The Reorganized Government resumed construction in 1862. Following the admission of West Virginia as its own state in 1863, the hospital was renamed the West Virginia Hospital for the Insane. The first patients were admitted in October 1864, but construction

continued into 1881. The 200-foot central clock tower was completed in 1871, and separate rooms for black people were completed in 1873. The hospital was intended to be self-sufficient, and a farm, dairy, waterworks, and cemetery were located on its grounds, which ultimately reached 666 acres in area. Its name was changed to Weston State Hospital in 1913.

Originally designed to house 250 patients in solitude, the hospital held 717 patients by 1880; 1,661 in 1938; over 1,800 in 1949; and, at its peak, 2,600 in the 1950s in overcrowded conditions. A 1938 report by a group of North American medical organizations found that the hospital housed "epileptics, alcoholics, drug addicts and non-educable mental defectives" among its population. A series of reports by The Charleston Gazette in 1949 found poor sanitation and insufficient furniture, lighting, and heating in much of the complex, while one wing, which had been rebuilt using Works Progress Administration funds following a 1935 fire started by a patient, was comparatively luxurious.

By the 1980s, the hospital had a reduced population due to changes in the treatment of mental illness. Those patients that could not be controlled were often locked in cages. In 1986, the Governor announced plans to build a new psychiatric facility elsewhere and to convert the Weston hospital to a prison. In May 1994, the new facility was built, and the old Weston State Hospital was closed. The building and its grounds have since been mostly vacant. In 1999, all four floors of the interior of the building were damaged by several city and county police officers playing paintball, three of whom were dismissed over the incident.

The hospital was auctioned by the West Virginia Department of Health and Human Resources on August 29, 2007. In October 2007, a Fall Fest was held at the Weston State Hospital. Guided daytime tours were offered, as well as a haunted hospital tour at night, a haunted hayride and a treasure hunt starting on the hospital front porch.

The owners now offer historic tours and daytime paranormal tours six days-a-week, Ghost Tours on Friday nights, and Ghost Hunts (which last all night) on Saturday nights.

Throughout its history, the Arrowhead Hotel had served the destitute families associated with the Trans-Allegheny Lunatic Asylum. At times, it catered to patients and their kin. At others, its residents were associates of the staff, who themselves drifted into cruelty from internalizing the facility's penal code. Of course, the town of Arrowhead had its troubles, too. Being founded as the subordinate neighbor to wealth fomented its own discontent, a tragic dynamic driven by the duress of poverty, hopelessness, and vice spread across generations. At irregular intervals, the Arrowhead Hotel had feigned salvation for local denizens by serving as a speakeasy, a brothel, and an opium den.

§

Weeks passed, the days getting longer and the temperatures hospitable once again. Fires caught in the sugar shacks around town. I took up running to get fresh air. The pounding footfalls and active solitude kept my mind at bay. The self-inflicted fatigue helped me sleep better, too. Though I relearned every outing that you can't run away from yourself.

For our intents and purposes, the exhibition opening was a success. The gallerist and I packed his venue with artists, friends, and patrons. My work pleased those who knew what to expect and confused many more, pleasurably ruffling some feathers. We drank all the wine and finished the cheese. We made good sales, too. A group of us took it to the bar after, celebrating with whiskey and the jukebox. I wasn't tired when I got home, so I went online to buy myself a watch with the windfall from the show. I couldn't decide on my favorite model, so I had a black *Nishat*, a blue *Janata*, and a white *Pilot* shipped out from Mumbai. And then I passed out.

A buzz had developed in town over the month-long run of the show. Attendance was consistent and strong. I stopped by once a week to chat, tripping over the pack of strays that started hanging out on the block. A collarless Doberman tried to sneak in the door as I entered the gallery. My friend was high on a ladder, tweaking the track lighting. I was lucky to have caught him, he said. He needed to make a run to town—the electric had been acting up and he was constantly swapping out bulbs. A tech was coming to inspect the system later in the day. I scratched my belly as I listened.

Turns out all three watches came broken, so I knifed-off their bands and hung them on a leather strap around my neck. Each told a different story—one dented, one frozen, one sprinting. All of them itched.

The gallerist reviewed our sales from the show. The strongest works had been claimed at the opening. The lesser drawings were moving too, making it a profitable venture for us both. I smirked, feeling the savvy capitalist, having flipped those crap frames for cold, hard cash. Initially, all I wanted was to get them out of the house. But the longer they were with me, the more I knew they demanded longer life. Cleaning them was nothing nice. The paper and the mats were tacky as I peeled them from the frames. The residual wetness made burning the prints difficult. I kneeled above them, stoking the flame with deep breaths. I coughed out lungfulls of the bitter smoke, my body rocking above the miniature pyre. But it was all worth it in the end. Now I had money. Fuckin-a right. Suckers—the frames live on. With their buyers. With you. They still have more to give.

I ran the windshield wipers as I started up the truck. The spray didn't activate until the blades had made one pass, arcing some freshly dropped bird shit into a brown-grey smear through my vision. Where'd these ravens come from? I've got to pay closer attention. I counted my money another time, folding it in half as the blue fluid streaked down the glass. I turned up the radio and cracked the glove box. The cash rotated once in the air before nesting against the barrel of my GLOCK. I called the neighbors from my cell and left a voicemail for their kids, trading twenty bucks against their feeding the dog until I returned. I rubbed my eyes and rolled towards the highway. I laughed. It was all downhill to Arrowhead.

adamablue.com

www.ingramcontent.com/pod-product-compliance
Lightning Source LLC
Chambersburg PA
CBHW050815180526
45159CB00004B/1676